THE STAR-SPANGLED BANANA

and Other Revolutionary Riddles

compiled by **Charles Keller and Richard Baker**

Illustrated by **Tomie de Paola**

Prentice-Hall, Inc., Englewood Cliffs, N.J.

Printed in the United States of America ·J

Prentice-Hall International, Inc., London
Prentice-Hall of Australia, Pty. Ltd.,
North Sydney
Prentice-Hall of Canada, Ltd., Toronto
Prentice-Hall of India Private Ltd., New Delhi
Prentice-Hall of Japan, Inc., Tokyo

Book design by Dann Jacobus and Tomie de Paola

Library of Congress Cataloging in Publication Data

Keller, Charles.
   The star spangled banana and other revolutionary riddles.

   SUMMARY: Riddles based on the American Revolution and other events and personalities from America's early history.
   1. Riddles--Juvenile literature. 2. United States --History--Revolution--Miscellanea. [1. Riddles. 2. United States--History--Revolution] I. Baker, Richard, joint author. II. De Paola, Thomas Anthony, illus. III. Title.
PN6371.5.K4   398.6   74-594
ISBN 0-13-842971-5

What was the first bus to cross the Atlantic?

Columbus.

Why were the Indians the first ones in this country?

Because they had reservations.

Why did the Indian wear feathers?

To keep his wigwam.

How did the Mayflower show affection for America?

It hugged the shore.

What ship came to America a month before the May-flower?

The April Shower.

What were the 100 animals that came to this country on the Mayflower?

Ninety-eight rabbits and two turkeys.

What happened to the Pilgrim when an Indian shot at him?

He had an arrow escape.

Why was the first Thanksgiving day turkey like a ghost?

It was a goblin.

Where did the first corn come from?

The stalk brought it.

What kind of music did the Pilgrims dance to?

Plymouth Rock.

If William Penn's aunts kept a pastry shop, what would they call their prices?

The pie rates of Penn's aunts.

Who introduced the pendulum to America?

Pendulum Franklin

Was Benjamin Franklin surprised when the lightning hit the key on his kite?

He found it shocking.

Why did Benjamin Franklin discover electricity?

So he could use his electric can opener.

What was purple and ruled the waves?

Grape Britain.

Why was the Stamp Act repealed after just one year?

The colonists licked it.

What did they do at the Boston Tea Party?

I don't know. I wasn't invited.

Why was a vote of the Continental Congress like a bad cold?

Because sometimes the eyes have it and sometimes the nose.

Where was the Declaration of Independence signed?

At the bottom.

What is the difference between the Declaration of Independence and a cat?

One has pauses at the end of its clauses, the other has claws at the end of its paws.

If one signal was by land and two if by sea, what were three and four?

Seven.

Why was Paul Revere just like a penny?

He was the one sent.

What went all the way from Concord to Lexington without moving an inch?

The highway.

Why did Paul Revere ride his horse from Boston to Lexington?

Because it was too heavy to carry.

Who owned the smallest radio station in colonial times?

Paul Revere. He broadcast from one plug.

What American patriot was the easiest to see through?

Thomas Paine.

How did the Whigs attempt to keep the revolution a secret?

By not telling Tories.

To what man did the minutemen take off their hats?

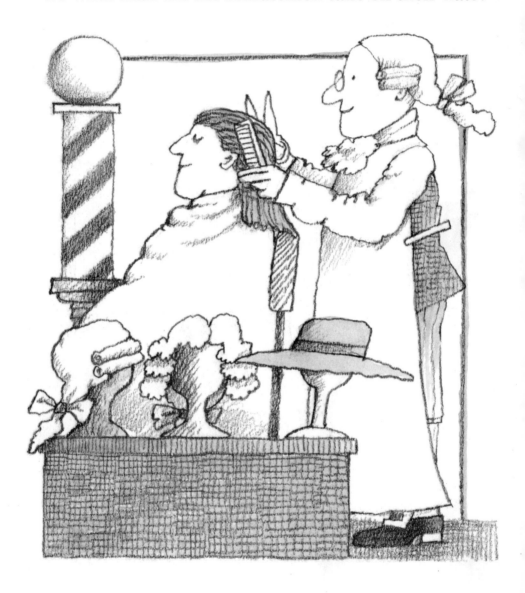

The barber.

Why were the ladies so fond of American army men?

Because every lady likes a good offer, sir.

What were the turning points in Boston's history during the Revolutionary War?

Street corners.

In colonial times what was the difference between gun-powder and facepowder?

One went off with a bang and the other went on with a puff.

What length were women's skirts in colonial times?

A little above two feet.

What did the American navy do when the British ships came at them as thick as peas?

Shell them, of course.

Why didn't they play cards on the Bon Homme Richard?

Because John Paul Jones stood on the deck.

Why is the Liberty Bell like a joke?

They're both cracked.

Why was the Liberty Bell so discreet?

It never spoke until it was tolled.

What was Betsy Ross' reply when she was asked if the flag was ready?

Give me a minute, man.

What did they call Betsy Ross when they didn't know her name?

Mrs. Sew and Sew.

When crossing the Delaware, why did George Washington stand up in the boat?

Because if he sat down they would have given him an oar.

When is a piece of wood like the King of England?

When it is a ruler.

Why was the King of England like a book?

Because he had a title.

Which king of England had a sour disposition?

George the Pickle.

For what was George II chiefly responsible?

George III.

What ghost haunted the palace of George III?

The spirit of 76.

What was the difference between George III's first son and a frisbee?

One is heir to the throne and the other is thrown in the air.

Why was King George III like a cloudy day?

He was reigning at the time.

Why did George Washington chop down the cherry tree?

It stumps me.

Why didn't George Washington's father spank him when he chopped down the cherry tree?

George still had the axe in his hand.

What did George Washington's father say when he saw his report card?

George, you're going down in history.

Why was Washington's army so tired on April 1?

They had just finished a march of 31 days.

Why did the soldiers whisper in the stable?

Because horses carry tails.

On a cold winter day at Valley Forge what did Washington's troops have on hand?

Gloves.

If George Washington were alive today, why couldn't he throw a silver dollar across the Potomac?

Because a dollar doesn't go as far as it used to.

Who did Martha Washington give her handkerchief to?

The town crier.

What does Washington D. C. stand for?

Washington, Daddy of his Country.

What is red, white and blue and covered with polka dots?

Uncle Sam with measles.

What is red, white and blue and yellow all over?

The Star Spangled Banana.

What made Francis Scott Key famous?

He knew all the verses to the Star Spangled Banner.

What is red, white and blue and smells?

A Yankee Doodle Dandelion.

When did they first say, "God Bless America?"

When it sneezed.

Why is it against the law to shoot our National Bird
if it is not feeling well?

Because it would be an ill-eagle act.

MARSH
MALLOWS